A Heart's Song

Erika Cartwright

BookLeaf Publishing

A Heart's Song © 2022 Erika Cartwright

Presentation by *BookLeaf Publishing*

Web: www.bookleafpub.com

E-mail: info@bookleafpub.com

ISBN: 9789395969529

First edition 2022

DEDICATION

In loving memory of Erika and Theo Hartmann, thank you for the stories, for your love, and the lessons you thought me along the way.

ACKNOWLEDGEMENT

To my great-aunt, Annelise, thank you for introducing me to books and the magic of fairy tales, you opened a new world for me.

A special thank you to my mother, Maria, you've always been my rock, there are no words to express the gratitude I feel. I love you mom.

To my father Fredrick, for your encouragement.

To my husband Seth, for listening to my writing, sometimes for hours, for your encouragement and support.

My brothers, Chris and John, and my beautiful children; Alexis, Natalie, Andrew, Nickolas, Cameron, and Seth Jr. you have always been my inspiration to see the beauty in the world around us.

To my granddaughter Ophelia, my newest inspiration, I can't wait to see who you will grow to be.

To my mother-in-law, Kay, thank you for believing in me when I didn't believe in myself.

To my father-in-law, Howard, thank you for choosing to be there for me, when you didn't have to be.

A special thank you to my friend Ronnie McDowell, for your encouragement and support.

To all the wonderful people in the Ronnie McDowell Fan-Family, thank you for your friendships and the wonderful stories you've shared with me over the years.

PREFACE

To me, poetry has always been a song of the heart. Poetry is a way to connect to others, to share experiences and feelings of happiness, love, and pain. It's a way to help deal with grief, or it can simply lift you up. Whatever your reason, may you find happiness and peace.

Tapestry of Time

Each life is a story,
a pattern of intricate design,
threads woven and entwined,
some touching only the briefest
moment in time

A unique pattern gently spun,
as each new story has begun,
threads in time, continue to wind,
quickly moving are the hands of time,
patterns of the grand design,
as new threads combine

Slowly spinning are the wheels of fate,
twisted and entwined,
nothing but shadows left behind,
threads cut short before their time,
are forever entwined,
a lasting imprint in the fabric of time

Souls Full of Light and Love

I look at the world with a heavy heart,
and wonder how we can each do our part.
Instead of standing against one another in a
world of chaos and discontent,
we should use our time well spent,
to stand up for those that can't
souls trapped in life's turbulent ocean,
 "it's sink or swim," they scream within!

There is but one conclusion,
We must see past the noise and confusion!
To step away from worldly disillusion
Look for the soul trapped within this temporary
shell,
Lend a helping hand, let hope grow and swell,
Open your heart and let love dwell!
We are on this earth for a short, short spell.
So why not love and live it well!

As part of His grand design, not a soul should be
left behind!
So, reach deep inside and come to realize,
we were all sent from Heaven above,
Souls full of light and love to live and learn.
Each given a chance to teach and guide

after the lessons, at the end of their turn, having shared
friendship, laughter, and tears, after hopefully many, many years.
we are called to return from whence we came
Let us not leave this world in shame!

This Memorial Day

From the days of civil war,
through modern times,
Let us honor those left behind,
those fallen before their time,
for freedom that's yours and mine

To honor the red, white, and blue,
For this is what our Heros' were called to do,
Men and women who paid the price,
of the ultimate sacrifice

Pick a Red poppy, and place it on that final site,
a reminder of the blood that was shed,
to think of all those who never made it back,
how we all wish it hadn't been their time.

A moment of silence is all I ask,
for the souls who were called home,
to serve with Heavens very best,
whisper a prayer, that it may lay on God's ear,
to bring comfort, healing, peace, and love
for all those who've lost way too much

This Memorial Day, let's wipe away the tears,
forever they're in our hearts to stay,
and look for the day that peace will come our
way,
Let's honor our Heros on this Memorial Day

Hidden Angels

There are hidden angels among us to teach and
guide,
to stand by our side, if only for a little while,
angels you can see,
you would never suspect they have been sent
to save you and me,

To touch our hearts in ways unseen,
from the laughter of a special child,
a shared memory from a foggy mind,
a homeless man's smile,
they touch our hearts and move our souls

With childlike wonder they view the world,
through struggle and pain, they carry on,
their faith remaining strong,
If our paths are meant to cross,
and one of these angels is sent from above,
remember to share kindness and love

Heavenly Places

When I feel down and out,
I look far beyond the clouds,
I close my eyes and let love in,
knowing I have friends in Heavenly places,
where the angels sing

With streets of gold and choirs too!
Heaven must have quite a view,
when I feel down and out,
I close my eyes and let love in,
Knowing one day I'll walk with Heaven's King

Many things to do,
many lessons to learn before it's my turn,
I smile and close my eyes and let love in,
Knowing I have friends in Heavenly places,
Where the angels sing

When my heart is heavy, my spirit weary,
when I can't see life's path clearly,
I smile and close my eyes and let love in,
knowing I have friends in Heavenly places,
where the angels sing

I must stay strong and carry on,
singing their song,
knowing I have friends in Heavenly places,
where the angels sing

Gumball Machine

My love begins at the gumball machine,
There she stands, a vision in a teenage dream
Over by the gumball machine,
Ponytail, mini skirt, white tank top,
Summer just got way too hot!
By the gumball machine,
By the gumball machine

Pretty as a picture, a high school queen,
Making me wish I were James Dean,
Cherry red lips, her smile so sweet,
She's all I need!
Over by the gumball machine,
By the gumball machine

Her friends stroll by, wave and say "hi"
A wiggle and a giggle,
A bubble and a pop!
There they stop,
By the gumball machine,
By the gumball machine

I lose my nerve,
About to give up,
Don't know if she's ready or not,
She grabs her sweater, turns to go,
It's now or never, better get ready and,go,go,go,
To the gumball machine,
The gumball machine

I gather my nerve,
Take a deep breath,
Get it together, just one more step,
To the gumball machine,
The gumball machine

I tap her shoulder,
She turns and smiles, oh so sweet,
My heart turns to butter,
My knees are weak,
I begin to sweat,
It's about to get better,
At the gumball machine,
The gumball machine

I take her hand,
I've got a question that just can't wait,
I begin to shake,
My high school ring I offer for her to take,
A promise I'm wanting to make,
By the gumball machine,
The gumball machine

Our love, our live began
by the gumball machine,
Now I hold her hand,
as our son walks in,
A giggle and a grin,
His teenage queen smiles at him,
There they go, hand in hand,
To the gumball machine,
The gumball machine

Thank You for Your Music, A Tribute to Ronnie McDowell and his Fan Family

After the show one evening, I went home to settle in. The stories I had heard while working the phone were running through my mind. As I sat there, I pondered the day's events and my mind started to wonder. I recalled so many conversations, the laughs and tears we have shared over the past years.

Many stories came to mind. Tales of over 50 years of Gospel, Country, and Rock'n Roll, stories filled with faith, friendship, family, loyalty, and love.

As well as stories of the day the world cried, as they heard the news" The King of Rock'n Roll, "had died. Tales of heartbreak and shock, so many shattered dreams. The pain ran deep, nations were left in disbelieve, and through tear filled eyes, the world said goodbye.

Among those turned away at Graceland's gates, A young man stood, unaware of what fate was about to share. It brought a smile to my eyes, as I thought of all the lives touched by music, especially by these two guys. Just when I began to doze, what was that, but the ringing phone? I rose and wiped the sleep from my eyes, I blinked in surprise as the caller ID, said, "Heaven." I found myself at the base of the old wooden staircase, in the lobby I saw them standing there, Ronnie and the man I'd seen hundreds of times, unaware of my presence it seemed. It was the voice I had recognized, and my eyes widened in surprise. I had heard it many times. In songs since I was 6 years old, and as I knew then it turned out to be life-long thing. I can't tell you how long they spoke of friends and family they had known, each shared stories of their own. Awestruck I listened as he spoke, "There were so many mourning in the chapels, as I watched with His hand in mine. Now I sing and play in my Father's house. George, Johnny, and June are picking a tune, old Pops grinning ear to ear as he became Heaven's trumpeter. Mama and Conway send their love, as for the rest, they all send their best" I imagined Heaven's ' music hall of fame and hoped all made it into the book by name. His laughter, warm and rich, after all he too was a baritone. "Now, you listen here," Stunned, I listened as he spoke," Some call it fate, some destiny. I saw that day, at Graceland's' gates how you were turned away, and to this day, I hope you'll say, that it was meant to be this way. I reached many in my time, yet I had to leave them all behind. I tried to spread his message with my songs, but I wasn't meant to have that long. Thank you for the words, and the songs you wrote, you healed their hearts and carried on. Thank you for doing your part, as you continue with your songs. Spread hope and love in times like these, let the music set you free."

More than a Token

What I wouldn't give for one more smile,
one more chance to kiss your lips,
To whisper words unsaid, truths left unspoken,
Our love was so much more than a token,
We were the ones others longed to be,
back when it was you and me,
Our song would play, we'd start to dance,
Under starry nights and summer skies,
Wrapped in your arms, safe and loved,
Until the day you said goodbye,
Shattered pieces of my bleeding heart,
Left my world falling apart,
Forever, once was spoken,
Yet fate had other plans,
I've come to find there's
nothing left but a token
of the love we once shared

Colors of Humanity

I'm asked what color defines me,
So I must sit, and ponder:
Do I say red?
Or do I go a step further than that?
Say black perhaps?
Should I go with yellow instead?
As strange as it may seem, even green?

Why these colors, you ask?
Let me explain.
Red for the blood that flows in all our veins,
Black for the pupils through which we see the world,
Green for my iris, a random color it seems,
Yellow, for the sun in my hair

Why not mention the color of my skin?
It doesn't define me,
It's just a temporary shell we're in,
We can let color define us,
Or we can let our differences unite us,
Step outside your norm,
Don't allow it to conform

Look around, and see a rainbow of humanity,
All uniquely beautiful in their own way,
It is because of this I dare say,
The color of humanity defines me

The Candle

I knew you'd say goodbye,
when you told me I was too petty to cry,
Shattered dreams and a broken heart,
it tore my world apart,
Yet the candle keeps on burning.

Long days and lonely nights,
wishing you were at my side,
Through tear filled eyes you said goodbye,
Yet the candle keeps on burning

As I try to hide away the pain,
I watch out the window at the pouring rain,
Nothing will remain the same,
Yet the candle keeps on burning

Forever my heart will continue yearning,
Until the day you'll be returning,
I'll keep the candle burning

My Best Friend

I look into your eyes and see only loyalty and
love,
I know in my heart,
you were sent from above,
To comfort me with love,
When the days are long,
And I don't know how to carry on

You make me smile, even through tear filled
eyes,
The walks we take,
Brighten my days,
You lift my mood,
and fill me with gratitude

I love the excitement you show,
As I come in the door,
You rush to me,
I nearly tumble to the floor,
Happy barks, and a wagging tail,
in your eyes I can never fail

The heavens knew I needed you,
For your heart is true,
I see your soul as I look into your eyes,
No use to disguise this gratitude I feel inside.

When you were sent,
I found my best friend,
Loyalty and love,
Sent from above,
to me you'll always be,
so much more than "just a pup"

Do you think of me?

Do you think of me, the way I do you?
I close my eyes, my mind wonders, and I see
your smile
When our eyes meet passions rise,
It's difficult to disguise,
this fire burning deep inside,
I long to be in your arms,
to taste your gentle kiss,
yet I can only wish

I wonder, do you think of me?
Do I dare ask what is in your heart?
Another time, another place,
a perfect pair we could have made,
What a cruel twist of fate,
That we should meet now,
This time, this place…

Storms inside

Lost in an ocean,
of simply not knowing,
Torment and confusion,
Trapped deep within disillusion

Raging storms, and rising tides,
Trapped from the world outside,
In darkness and fear,
Screams, no one seems to hear

Burning throats, heavy breaths,
Each seems harder than the last,
Not knowing where to turn,
As frantic emotions churn

Frightening thoughts, and breaking hearts,
feeling of being torn apart,
isolation and a false facade,
longing for a normal part

Raging storms inside,
for some they're easier to hide,
too many giving up the fight,
depression in the dark of night,
please hold on through the morning light

Seasons of our lives

Spring flowers of our youth,
everything is bright and new,
tender and true

Summer days of love and fun,
joys and heartaches just begun,
as we dance around the sun,

Changing Autumn leaves,
on bended knees,
as we search this world for peace,

Reminiscent Winter nights,
warm memories of days gone by,
We carry in our hearts,
Until the time we must depart,

Changing seasons of our lives,
cherish the gifts,
given through His sacrifice,
through each season of our lives

Memories

Silver moon light,
brightness the darkness,
crickets serenading,
slowly my heart starts aching

Yet, no longer is it breaking,
time stops fading,
memories of days long past,
fill my heart with gladness

When I close my eyes,
I'm taken back, scents and sounds,
so strong, wishing I could reach out to touch,
the days I miss so much

Simpler days in grandma's kitchen,
the love and laughter there,
nothing else can compare,
to knowing how much you cared

Childhood memories of family and friends,
of joys and lessons learned,
how I yearn to go back again,
to hold each one of them

Bitter sweet, memories are a treat,
a moment in time,
forever etched in your mind,
bring a smile to your heart and a tear to your eye

Gone but never forgotten,
I wish I could go back in time,
and hold you one more time,
just for a little while, to sit and talk,
perhaps, go for a walk as we did back then

The memories I carry in my heart,
let me know we're never truly apart,
you've always played such a big, big part,
you'd wipe away the tears and tell me not to cry,
and say it isn't really good-bye

I dry my eyes, put on a smile,
because just for a little while,
the memories reunited us,
and I could feel your love

Have No Fear

In a world of anger and hatred,
we walk often tempted by disillusion,
searching for answers in life's noise and confusion,
too blinded by fear to see our path clear

It's in these times we must stand tall,
look to the Heavens and answer our call,
every choice, affects us all,
resist worldly temptations,
let's help end suffering throughout the nations

Set aside our fear, and trust that He is near,
lend a helping hand,
come lets' take a stand for love and peace,
get down on bended knees,

Instead of division,
judge not, and look inside your heart,
so different we are not,
let love be your part

Help heal a broken heart,
feed the hungry, help the weak,
for those that cannot, you must speak,
be humble and kind, and have no fear,
knowing He is near

When you said goodbye

Dark clouds cover the sky,
Raindrops falling from my eyes,
Raging storms,
I feel inside,
since you said goodbye

Slamming doors and angry words,
No one left to hurt,
you promised you'd never leave,
I swore I wouldn't cry,
although I knew you'd say goodbye

I lock away my tears,
my heart aching for our happy years,
I hold my head up high,
after all, it was your choice to say goodbye

Time heals all wounds,
is what I'm told,
how I thought together we'd grow old,
now I've seen the truth unfold,
you have someone new to hold

I pretend my heart isn't breaking,
perhaps one day it will stop aching,
until then, I'll be strong,
with my head up high, I'll carry on,
after all, it was you that chose goodbye

Precious child

From the first time I looked into your eyes,
I knew you were mine to teach and guide,
A beautiful gift sent from above,
My precious child to love

Your tiny fingers gripping mine,
How I was filled with fright,
 as I stayed up most nights,
Just wanting to hold you tight

How each tear you cried,
simply tore me up inside,
Each passing year, you grew,
If only you knew the joy I feel inside,
as I look into your eyes

From your first breath,
through those tiny wabbly steps,
I've watched you grow,
my precious child how I wish you'd know,
the beauty of your soul

You Are

The gentle breeze brushes against my cheek,
I feel your touch,
I see you in the dancing leaves,
and I know you are here with me

You're the warmth of the sun on my face,
in the eyes of a child down by the lake,
I feel you in every breath that I take,
you float with the butterflies,
and wait with the birds, up on their perch

I feel your love as I walk through the valley,
and watch you soar high on the wings of the
eagles,
you're in the sweet fragrance of the wildflowers,
your loving embrace, I feel with every step I
take,
no matter how long my journey takes,
you are here to walk with me

I see you in the face of the homeless man down
the alley,
I feel you in the rain, as you take away the pain,
you comfort the lonely, and heal the broken,
You Are every word that is spoken.

Printed in the USA
CPSIA information can be obtained
at www.ICGtesting.com
LVHW011256020823
753722LV00019B/1537